Love
Canal

Other titles in the *American Disasters* series:

**The Challenger
Disaster**
Tragic Space Flight
ISBN 0-7660-1222-0

The Exxon Valdez
Tragic Oil Spill
ISBN 0-7660-1058-9

**Fire in Oakland,
California**
Billion-Dollar Blaze
ISBN 0-7660-1220-4

Hurricane Andrew
Nature's Rage
ISBN 0-7660-1057-0

The L.A. Riots
**Rage in the City
of Angels**
ISBN 0-7660-1219-0

**The Mighty
Midwest Flood**
Raging Rivers
ISBN 0-7660-1221-2

**Mount St. Helens
Volcano**
Violent Eruption
ISBN 0-7660-1552-1

**The Oklahoma City
Bombing**
**Terror in the
Heartland**
ISBN 0-7660-1061-9

**Plains Outbreak
Tornadoes**
Killer Twisters
ISBN 0-7660-1059-7

**San Francisco
Earthquake, 1989**
**Death and
Destruction**
ISBN 0-7660-1060-0

The Siege at Waco
Deadly Inferno
ISBN 0-7660-1218-2

The Titanic
Disaster at Sea
ISBN 0-7660-1557-2

TWA Flight 800
Explosion in Midair
ISBN 0-7660-1217-4

**The World Trade
Center Bombing**
Terror in the Towers
ISBN 0-7660-1056-2

Love Canal

Toxic Waste Tragedy

Victoria Sherrow

Enslow Publishers, Inc.

40 Industrial Road   PO Box 38
Box 398   Aldershot
Berkeley Heights, NJ 07922 Hants GU12 6BP
USA   UK

http://www.enslow.com

Library of Congress Cataloging-in-Publication Data

Sherrow, Victoria.
    Love Canal : toxic waste tragedy / Victoria Sherrow.
        p. cm. — (American disasters)
Includes bibliographical references and index.
    ISBN 0-7660-1553-X
    1. Chemical plants—Waste disposal—Environmental aspects—New York (State)—
Niagara Falls—Juvenile literature. 2. Hazardous waste sites—New York (State)—
Niagara Falls—Juvenile literature. 3. Love Canal Chemical Waste Landfill (Niagara
Falls, N.Y.)—Juvenile literature. [1. Love Canal Chemical Waste Landfill (Niagara Falls,
N.Y.) 2. Hazardous waste sites. 3. Pollution. 4. Environmental protection.]
I. Title. II. Series.
    TD181.N72 .N5137 2001
    363.738'4'0974798—dc21
                                                    00-009474

Printed in the United States of America

10 9 8 7 6 5 4 3 2 1

To Our Readers:
We have done our best to make sure all Internet addresses in this book were active and
appropriate when we went to press. However, the author and the publisher have no
control over and assume no liability for the material available on those Internet sites
or on other Web sites they may link to. Any comments or suggestions can be sent by
e-mail to comments@enslow.com or to the address on the back cover.

Illustration Credits: AP/Wide World Photos, pp. 1, 6, 8, 25, 29, 30, 32, 36, 39;
Bruce Coleman, Inc., pp. 10, 12, 14, 17, 19, 21, 22, 26, 28.

Cover Illustration: Bruce Coleman, Inc.

Contents

Mark Zanatian, one of the children endangered by the chemicals buried beneath his school in Love Canal, holds a banner during a protest meeting in August 1978.

CHAPTER 1

Backyard Hazards

On August 3, 1978, more than five hundred people crowded into a school auditorium. They lived in the Love Canal neighborhood of Niagara Falls, New York. Two days earlier, the state's health commissioner, Dr. Robert Whalen, had made a chilling statement. He said there was "a serious threat to health, safety, and welfare" in Love Canal.[1] An alarmed community had come to talk with public officials.

Months earlier, the people who lived in Love Canal had heard upsetting news. Their elementary school was built on top of a vast chemical dump. Hundreds of homes and another school had been built in this same area. Chemicals had been leaking into the sewer system and the soil for more than twenty years. Smelly black liquid seeped into basements. It bubbled up on the ground.

Homeowner Lois Gibbs was at the meeting that evening. She later recalled the deep fears people expressed. Gibbs wrote, "Some were worried and some were crying. . . The lady on the left was talking about her three-year-old, another about her unborn child, and another saying she wants to have children and is afraid."[2]

Events at Love Canal shocked Americans. Many people learned that toxic waste disposal was everyone's problem. It was a growing problem that needed long-term solutions.

These events scarred a region that had long been known for its scenic beauty. Niagara Falls had first become

Before the Love Canal disaster, the Niagara Falls region was most famous for being the "honeymoon capital of the world."

a famous tourist site and honeymoon spot in the 1800s. But things changed after 1978. A local teenager said grimly, "Niagara Falls is no longer the honeymoon capital but the toxic waste capital."[3]

Ironically, the man who gave Love Canal its name had dreamed of a "model city." William T. Love was a land developer. He planned to build a canal that would connect the upper and lower parts of the Niagara River. It would bring water around the 200-foot falls. This would produce hydroelectric power for homes and industry.

Workers began digging the canal in 1896. However, Love had to give up his canal project. Hard economic times hit America. People did not want to invest in Love's project. He was left with a hole about 3000 feet long, up to 20 feet deep, and almost 100 feet wide. The city of Niagara Falls bought the land at a public auction.

Local residents used the canal as a swimming hole in the summer. In winter, it became an ice rink. People called it "Love Canal." A man who grew up in Niagara Falls later said, "When we first moved there, the Love Canal was there and it was a beautiful body of water."[4]

In 1905, the Hooker Electrochemical Corporation (later called the Hooker Chemical and Plastics Corporation) set up a factory near the canal. Hooker went on to make industrial chemicals, plastics, fertilizers, and pesticides (substances that kill insects).

Few people lived near the old canal. Much of the soil in the area was clay. In the early 1940s, the city of Niagara Falls used part of the canal as a landfill. Hooker also dumped waste materials there. Some people said they saw U.S. Army trucks coming in and out in the late 1940s. But the army says it never put wastes in the canal.

As Hooker's business grew, it produced tons of wastes. The canal seemed like a good place to bury them.

*B*y August 1978, it had been determined that the chemicals beneath Love Canal were a threat to people's health.

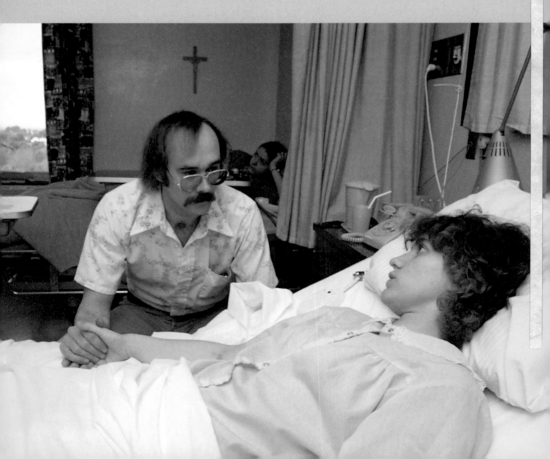

CHAPTER 2

Dumping Ground

In 1946, Hooker bought Love's unfinished canal. The company planned to use it as a dumpsite for chemical waste. Waste or by-products are left over when factories produce plastic, fertilizer, and other materials.

Hooker dammed off the upper end of the canal and drained the water. The company then put wastes into this empty area. Some chemicals were dumped directly into the site. Others were stored in metal containers or fiber drums. These containers could wear out or break over time.

The Environmental Protection Agency (EPA) regards some waste products as health hazards. The EPA was created in 1970. Its jobs include making and enforcing laws concerning pollution and waste disposal. But the EPA did not yet exist when Hooker bought Love's canal.

The EPA now divides hazardous wastes into six types. Toxic wastes (poisonous chemicals) can cause various health problems, even death. Corrosive wastes (for example, acids) eat away at metal, skin, and other

*T*he Hooker Chemical Corporation started dumping metal containers full of dangerous chemical wastes into the canal in 1946.

materials. Ignitable wastes can catch fire. Reactive wastes may explode or release deadly gases. This occurs when they become hot or are mixed with water or other substances. Radioactive wastes send out rays that can damage human cells. Such wastes can injure chromosomes (the genetic material inside the cells). Infectious wastes contain disease-causing organisms.

Over the years, Hooker dumped more than 42 million pounds of waste. These wastes were mostly toxic, ignitable, and corrosive. Some were pesticides that are known as carcinogens. These are substances that can cause cancer. Among them were four million pounds of chlorobenzenes. Benzene can cause blood cancers and other serious blood diseases. The canal also held several hundred pounds of dioxin, a powerful weed killer. Exposure to dioxin may cause nerve damage, cancer, and various diseases. Just a few ounces could kill millions of people.

Residents did not know exactly what was in the canal. But some people saw flames shooting up from the ground. People also heard explosions. Children still swam in parts of the canal where Hooker was not dumping wastes.

Hooker closed the dumpsite in 1953. The company later said it covered the site with hard-packed clay to keep out rain, added topsoil, and planted grass.

Meanwhile, more families had moved to Niagara Falls. The school board needed cheap land for a new elementary school. The board offered to buy the sixteen acres that included the dumpsite. Hooker agreed to sell the land in 1953. The school board paid the company a token $1. That year, Hooker took an income tax deduction for donating land to the city. Hooker later claimed it had not wanted to sell.

The property deed contained a warning for future owners. Hooker said that the canal "has been filled . . . with waste products resulting from the manufacturing of chemicals by [Hooker]."[1] The deed did not describe these toxic chemicals, however. Hooker did show school board members the dumpsite. Company officials also claim they warned people that the land should not be dug up.

Hooker claimed it had no further legal responsibility for the dump. The deed said the school board could not make Hooker pay "for injury to a person or persons, including death . . . or loss of or damage to property caused by, in connection with or by reason of the presence of said industrial wastes."[2]

Workers began building the school. Machines dug into the ground. The workers found what they called "a pit filled with chemicals."[3] They had broken the clay covering the dumpsite. The city then moved the school's location. They placed it eighty-five feet off to the side.

The 99th Street School opened in 1955. Each year, it enrolled between four hundred and five hundred children.

*T*his photo shows an aerial view of the dumpsite. By 1976, there were about 800 homes surrounding the site and a housing project with about 240 apartments.

Some of them played in the swampy field over the old canal. A former student, Barbara Quimby, later recalled one of these play areas. She and her friends called it "quicksand lagoon."[4] Quimby said, "We had special shoes which we kept in our garages to wear over there, because once you wore something, a pair of sneakers or whatever, you couldn't get them clean again."[5]

Real-estate developers bought land from the city. They built new homes in Love Canal. The city added sewers and another school. By 1976, there were about eight hundred small, one-family homes in the area. Some yards backed up to the old dump. Nearby, the LaSalle housing project held about two hundred and forty apartments.

Few new homeowners knew about the dumpsite. It looked like a normal grassy field. In fact, sales agents told them the city planned to build a park there.

Like millions of other people, these residents worked hard to buy their homes. They thought Love Canal was a fine place to live. Homeowner Lois Gibbs later wrote, "It was a lovely neighborhood in a quiet residential area, with lots of trees and lots of children outside playing. It seemed just the place for our family."[6]

CHAPTER 3

Fear and Anger

Even in the 1950s, people noticed danger signs at Love Canal. Some homeowners smelled foul chemical odors outdoors. Their basements stank, too. Pools of dark liquid from the swampy fields flowed into nearby yards. Pets that roamed outdoors lost patches of hair. Some pets came home with strange burns on their paws.

Three children playing in the schoolyard suffered chemical burns in 1959. Their parents told the school board. The city put dirt or clay over some of the muddy sections. Hooker later claimed that it had warned the school board to keep children away from certain areas.

In 1965, Joey Bulka was playing in the area the children called the "lagoon." He fell into a pit. Some muddy liquid dripped into Joey's ear. It burned a hole in his eardrum. His parents complained to the school board and the local health department. Mr. Bulka later said, "We called every day. They did absolutely nothing."[1]

More problems arose during the 1970s. Smelly slime

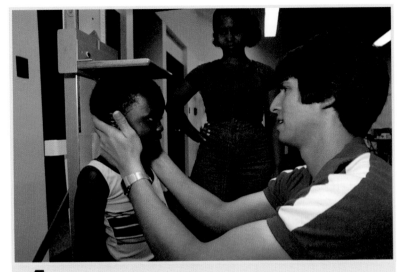

A doctor examines a child resident of Love Canal. Burns, rashes, and respiratory illness were the most common ailments exhibited by people in Love Canal.

oozed through basement walls. It dripped from the drains at the community swimming pool. Trees died. Many homeowners could not grow lawns or gardens. The vegetables that did grow were hard. They had strange shapes. Some people felt sick after eating them.

People also suffered skin burns and rashes. Some had breathing problems or chronic allergies. Anne Hillis later described her infant son's ongoing health problems. Hillis said, "[He] developed rashes, frequent bouts of diarrhea and respiratory problems—always respiratory problems."[2] Some residents did not know that many of their neighbors had similar problems. At the time, people were not as aware of environmental hazards. They didn't consider that there might be something wrong with their water or their land.

Rain and snow made things worse in Love Canal. In 1971, a blizzard caused major flooding. More storage drums burst and rose above the ground. The chemical smell got worse during heavy spring rains. One home-owner recalled those times: "You couldn't stand on the basement stairs—your eyes would water."[3] Some residents put in special pumps to keep their basements dry. Black sludge came into the pumps. It ate holes in the metal.

In October 1976, reporter David Pollak wrote a story about Love Canal for the *Niagara Gazette.* He described the history of the dumpsite and the land sale to the school board. He wrote about complaints from area home-owners.[4] Pollak and other reporters continued writing about Love Canal in 1976 and early 1977.

By 1977, many people had complained to city officials and the Hooker Company. The city hired an engineering firm to study the problem. The firm, Calspan, issued a report in August 1977. The report noted that broken drums were leaking chemicals into the ground. Polluted liquid had spread into storm sewers and basement pumps. Polychlorinated biphenyl (PCB) was found in storm sewers to the west of the canal. PCB can cause severe irritation in the nose, lungs, and skin. It might also contribute to birth defects if pregnant women are exposed to it. Scientists also found toxic chemicals in samples of groundwater and surface water.[5]

The International Joint Commission is an organization that keeps track of conditions in the Great Lakes. In 1976, the commission found traces of insecticide in Lake Ontario fish. It reported these findings to the governments of the United States and Canada. One source of this insecticide was the dumpsite at Love Canal.

In 1977, reporter Michael Brown began writing a series

New York state officials inspect a neighborhood in Love Canal.

of articles about Love Canal for the *Niagara Gazette*. He wrote that people living between 97th and 99th streets had chemicals flowing into their basements. Brown described the property damage and health problems in these homes. He described the cleanup plan Calspan had given to the city.[6]

Congressman John LaFalce represented the district of New York that included Niagara Falls. LaFalce met with residents and inspected the dumpsite. So did officials from the federal EPA. In October 1977, a local EPA official wrote to the EPA's toxic substances coordinator. Part of his memo said,

> There is no easy or quick solution to this problem because if you go about it in a temporary way it will continue to pop up. . . . If you go full out, a cleanup will cost a considerable amount. What to do with or how to treat the waste after it is removed may present a major problem.[7]

The *Niagara Gazette* carried more articles about Love Canal in April 1978. Michael Brown wrote about some of the chemicals in the dumpsite. He listed the health problems they might cause.

That same month, the New York State Health Department visited people's homes. They took air and soil samples from the basements. The state health commissioner, Robert Whalen, ordered the Niagara County Health Department to fence in the dumpsite and to remove all exposed chemicals.

Lois Gibbs grew alarmed as she read these reports. Her family lived on 101st Street. Her son attended the 99th

Street School. Michael Gibbs had been healthy before he started kindergarten in 1977. Then he developed skin rashes and his face swelled. He said his eyes hurt. In December 1977, he started having seizures. Tests showed that his white blood cell count was below normal. White blood cells are vital in helping the body fight off disease.

Gibbs decided the 99th Street School was dangerous. Michael's pediatrician and the family doctor sent letters to city officials. They asked to transfer Michael to another

*I*n addition to other symptoms, many people in Love Canal complained of headaches, stomach problems, and lung and kidney diseases.

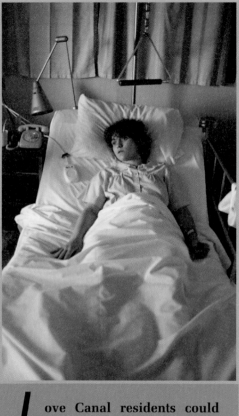

*L*ove Canal residents could not be sure just how much their health had been affected by the buried chemicals.

school. The superintendent of schools refused. Lois Gibbs later wrote,

He said Michael could not be removed from the school . . . because the statements alleged that the area was contaminated. If the area were contaminated, then it wasn't only Michael who should be removed; all the children should be removed. The superintendent said that he did not believe the area was contaminated, and, finally, that they were not about to close the 99th Street school.[8]

Gibbs decided to fight this decision. She later wrote, "I wasn't going to send my child to a place that was poisoned. . . . I thought that I, as a person, had rights, that I ought to have a choice."[9]

Gibbs launched a door-to-door campaign to shut down the school. Other residents signed her petition. They wrote down problems they thought were related to the dumpsite. People complained of chronic headaches, kidney diseases and bleeding, liver problems, stomach problems, and lung cancer. A few children had died of rare diseases. Their parents now wondered if the dumpsite was to blame.

Some women who moved to Love Canal had miscarriages (failed pregnancies) or abnormal babies even though their earlier pregnancies had been normal. Gibbs later said, "The more I heard, the more frightened I became. This problem involved much more than the 99th Street school. The entire community seemed to be sick!"[10]

Other people were also working with local and state officials to settle these issues. Residents wanted to know how the chemicals could affect them. Nobody seemed to know. The effects of all these chemicals had never been carefully studied. The situation at Love Canal was even more complex because there were so many different chemicals.

People became more and more upset. They criticized Hooker for creating the toxic dumpsite. They blamed the city for building schools and homes there.

Some people wanted to move, but they could not afford to. Most families could not buy another house unless they sold their present home for a fair price. People felt trapped in a toxic nightmare.

CHAPTER 4

"I Don't Want to Live Here"

People in Love Canal grew more worried during the summer of 1978. News reports increased their fears. One such story appeared in *The New York Times* on August 2, 1978. It was titled "Upstate Waste Site May Endanger Lives."

That day, the state health department held a meeting in Albany, the state capital. Health Commissioner Robert Whalen said the state planned to close the 99th Street School and clean up the yard. He warned people not to go in their basements. He told them not to eat food from their gardens. Pregnant women and children under age two were urged to leave Love Canal. Whalen said, "Love Canal is a great and imminent peril to the health of the general public."[1]

Lois Gibbs attended that meeting. She was glad the school would be closed. But Gibbs was upset that the state thought only certain people should move out. If Love Canal was dangerous for them, what about everyone else? Angrily, she asked Whalen, "What do you think you're doing?"[2]

The officials admitted they did not have all the answers. They said they needed to do more studies. They asked residents to send them health reports.

The next day, crowds gathered on the streets of Love Canal. Thomas Heisner had organized this rally. He told a reporter, "I can't sell the house. I can't give it away. I know people that won't even visit the house."[3] To the crowd, Heisner said, "Our homes are worthless. They're less than worthless."[4]

*T*imothy Schroeder's children play in front of his home in August 1978. Schroeder was one of many angry home-owners whose property was over the chemical dump.

Hundreds of people burned their mortgage papers and property tax bills in a trash can. They refused to pay taxes to a government they thought had betrayed them.

State officials came to a meeting at the 99th Street School the next night. Homeowners expressed confusion and anger. They wanted to know how to protect their health. Many wanted the government to help them leave Love Canal.

Rows of homes were boarded up and abandoned after the discovery of the chemical waste dump buried under Love Canal.

On August 4, residents formed the Love Canal Homeowners' Association (LCHA). They elected Lois Gibbs as president.

Gibbs later wrote that the LCHA set four main goals. The first goal was to "get all the residents . . . who wanted to be evacuated, evacuated and relocated, especially during the construction and repair of the canal."[5] Next, they wanted to protect the value of their homes. Third, they hoped to "get the canal fixed properly."[6] Their fourth goal was to "have air sampling and soil and water testing done throughout the whole area."[7]

Many homeowners looked to the LCHA for help. Other people joined different community groups that were working on the same problems. Sometimes there was friction between the LCHA and the other groups.

The LCHA found lawyers to help them. People who had serious health problems filed lawsuits against both the city and the Hooker company.

Meanwhile, local churches formed the Ecumenical Task Force to help residents. Sister Margeen Hoffman served as executive director. In August 1979, the Ecumenical Task Force helped hundreds of residents find temporary housing. The task force also provided meals, transportation, and other things.

Newspapers around the country called Love Canal the worst environmental disaster in decades. In Washington, D.C., Congressman LaFalce and Senators Jacob Javits and Daniel Patrick Moynihan of New York asked for federal aid.

*M*any families relocated after the discovery of the dangerous chemicals under Love Canal.

On August 5, 1979, President Carter declared Love Canal a federal disaster area. The federal government agreed to give New York $20 million to buy the homes of people who lived within two blocks of the old dumpsite. This meant that 239 families could leave.

Homeowner Thomas Heisner heard the news from Congressman LaFalce, who spoke to a large meeting of residents. Heisner said, "Up until now, I had lost the American vision and dream. The city ruined that vision."[8]

The government was used to helping victims of floods, hurricanes, and other natural disasters. Love Canal was a new kind of disaster. In fact, it was the first time the nation had declared an environmental disaster.

Love Canal also sparked a new kind of lawsuit. In 1979, the U.S. Department of Justice filed a complaint against Hooker. Another suit was filed against the city of Niagara Falls. Both the health department and the board of education were named in this lawsuit.

The Justice Department demanded that Hooker clean up the dumpsite. The federal government also sought millions of dollars as repayment for the money it was spending at Love Canal. The lawsuit also asked for money for medical research.

Still, the government was only helping one-fourth of the residents to leave Love Canal. People outside the area from 97th to 99th Street claimed they were also at risk. The LCHA carried out its own health survey of those 710 families. Dr. Beverly Paigen was a cancer research scientist at Roswell Park Memorial Institute in Buffalo. She helped the residents gather information and analyze the results.

*N*ew York Senator Daniel Patrick Moynihan was one of several politicians to request federal aid for the residents of Love Canal in 1978.

The LCHA study showed above-normal rates of miscarriages, stillbirths, crib deaths,

By October 1978, this foundation was all that was left of Thomas Heisner's Love Canal home. The family moved the entire house to another section of the city.

and diseases of the nervous system and urinary tract. The highest number of disorders occurred in homes located over old streambeds.[9] Dr. Paigen also studied children who lived in Love Canal. She found they had higher-than-normal rates of learning disabilities, seizure disorders, eye and skin irritations, and severe stomach pains.[10]

Homeowners who remained in Love Canal felt like victims. In April 1979, Anne Hillis spoke to a Senate committee. She told them, "Our homes are valueless, we can't sell, who would buy a home like this?"[11] One night at 2 A.M., Hillis found her young son crying under the living room couch. He said, "I don't want to live here anymore—I know that you will be sick again and I'll be sick again."[12] Another homeowner said people in Love Canal were "worried, sick and very disappointed with our government that is supposed to be out there working for the people and not against us."[13]

The state government agreed to remove some residents temporarily. A year later, hundreds of Love Canal residents were still living in motels or other temporary housing. LCHA members marched in protest along the streets near their Love Canal office during the spring of 1980. Some were arrested. Their leaders continued to make their case to public officials and in the media.

One couple wrote an emotional letter to the editor of the *Niagara Gazette* on April 27, 1980. It read in part:

> Every mother in the Love Canal is scared to death, wondering who will be the next one with leukemia symptoms. Will it be her child, her neighbor's child or even herself? Every family watches and wonders what the spring thaw is washing to the surface, scared of what their children might be walking in, playing in, or falling in. Is it dioxin? Or something worse?[14]

Fears rose when people heard the results of their blood tests. The EPA had asked them to take the tests. Lab results showed abnormally high rates of chromosome damage. Chromosomes are the material inside cells that carry traits from one generation to another.

Tensions kept rising at Love Canal. On May 19, 1980, angry residents held two EPA officials hostage. These men were kept from leaving the LCHA offices. LCHA members demanded that President Carter declare another national emergency. The EPA officials were released after six hours.

New York Governor Hugh Carey asked for federal money to permanently relocate the remaining families. He said, "My first concern is to relieve the level of anxiety and tension in those families."[15] Carey claimed that this kind of fear led to "a unique emergency situation which requires a unique federal response."[16]

President Carter first declared Love Canal a federal disaster area on August 5, 1979. It was the first time the United States had declared an environmental disaster.

On May 21, 1980, President Carter did declare a second federal emergency at Love Canal. At last, the remaining families could sell their homes to the government. They were told they would receive the "fair market value."

By then, the EPA had identified more than four hundred chemicals in Love Canal. Some chemicals were present in levels more than 5,000 times what was considered safe.[17]

People around the country heard about these dramatic events. They wondered if their neighborhoods were at risk, too. Americans learned there were tens of thousands of hazardous waste sites around the world.

Researchers found that certain kinds of neighborhoods were unfairly burdened with toxic dumps. Dumpsites were often placed in communities where people had lower incomes and lower education levels.

There were no federal programs for cleaning up toxic sites. The public demanded action. Love Canal resident Marie Pozniak asked a Senate committee to act quickly. She said, "We need to immediately pass laws and form agencies who can and will take on the responsibilities of finding and cleaning up these dump sites."[18]

CHAPTER 5

"A Black Cloud"

Congress responded to concerns about toxic wastes raised by events at Love Canal. It passed the Comprehensive Environmental Response Compensation and Liability Act of 1980. This became known as the "Superfund Law." It set up a 1.6-billion-dollar fund for toxic waste cleanups and emergencies. The law also encouraged research into safer ways to handle hazardous wastes and to reduce toxic waste production.

The Superfund Law requires the EPA to identify dumpsites that threaten health. These sites are placed on the National Priorities List. The law states that polluters will pay the cleanup costs, if possible.

Critics say the Superfund program has moved too slowly. In turn, the EPA says they have found far more toxic dumpsites than they expected. They have also faced many problems trying to clean them up. Also, the agency has suffered from leadership problems.

In 1986, Congress passed a new environmental law,

the Emergency Planning and Community Right-to-Know Act. The act describes plans to help communities cope with environmental disasters. It requires companies to report which hazardous materials they use. They must also reveal what amounts are released into the environment.

Some companies try to get around tougher regulations. Some have even dumped chemicals illegally. Government agents look into charges of illegal dumping. People who break the laws may be fined and sent to prison.

By 1990, the EPA had 1,207 dumpsites on the National Priorities List. Between 1980 and 1991, only thirty-four sites were removed from the list. During Bill Clinton's presidency, the EPA took on more than thirty cleanups each year. But in 1995, Congress let a tax on chemical and oil companies expire. This money had helped to pay for Superfund programs. A lack of funding halted some planned cleanups as of 1996. More than a thousand sites remained on the list as of 2000.

Cleanup efforts at Love Canal took several years. The state fenced in the most hazardous area. It posted signs that read: "Danger! Keep Out!"

Workers dug a trench system around the old canal. Underground contaminated water was pumped to a treatment facility. A clay cap was placed over the contaminated soil. The cap was meant to block out rain and keep chemicals out of the air.

Cleaning up this ten-block area cost more than

*I*n April 2000, the 93rd Street School became the last building to be demolished due to the Love Canal disaster. This site is now reserved as park space in the revitalized area.

$250 million. Even more money was spent cleaning the soil from the sewers and streambeds.

Questions remained about how Love Canal affected people's health. Some scientists said there was no proof that the toxic chemicals had caused health problems. Others argued that chemicals were surely to blame for so many miscarriages, birth defects, and other diseases. More studies were done during the 1980s. A new five-year study of former residents began in 1997. Scientists hope this study will give them important information.

European scientists have done similar studies. Researchers studied people living near twenty-one chemical landfills. Women who lived within three kilometers of these dumps were 33 percent more likely to have babies with birth defects.

Legal actions involving Love Canal dragged on for years. In 1985, some Love Canal residents settled a lawsuit with Hooker Chemical. They received $20 million. In 1994, New York State settled its lawsuit against Occidental Chemical Company, the company that then owned Hooker. Occidental agreed to pay $98 million. The next year, the U.S. government also settled its case against Occidental. The company offered the government $129 million. This amount was meant to pay for the costs of the cleanup and for relocating families.

Attorney General Janet Reno said, "Under the Superfund Law, the taxpayers are going to recover every dime that was spent."[1] Reno urged that the Superfund Law remain strong. She said, "If Congress will give us the resources, we will work to get polluters to pay their fair share."[2]

Lois Gibbs became known as the "Mother of the Superfund." She moved to Washington, D.C., and founded the Citizen's Clearinghouse for Hazardous Waste. The group later changed its name to Center for Health, Environment, and Justice (CHEJ). CHEJ has helped thousands of local citizens groups deal with toxic wastes. CHEJ helps people understand environmental laws and research.

In 1988, the New York State Department of Health declared that parts of Love Canal were "habitable"—fit for humans to live in. The sixteen-acre section around the dumpsite remained off-limits. The government said they would test the air, water, and soil from time to time.

A group funded by the government repaired dozens of homes outside the fenced-in area. The restored neighborhood was renamed "Black Creek Village." These homes were offered for sale at prices 15 to 20 percent below market prices for similar homes. Every home was sold. The buyers said they felt safe. One woman said, "I know what's in my backyard. Do you know what's in yours?"[3] Another new resident said, "This area has been tested and tested and tested."[4]

Some of these buyers had once lived in Love Canal. They chose to return. But other former residents said the area could never be proven safe. Luella Kenny's son Jon died of kidney disease at age seven before the family left Love Canal. Some people blame his death on exposure to chemicals at the dumpsite. Luella Kenny said, "The children are what bother me when I see them running around this neighborhood. I'm so frightened for them."[5]

A 1998 movie, "A Civil Action," brought more people's attention to toxic wastes. The movie focused on several families in Woburn, Massachusetts, who had fought an eight-year legal battle. They said polluted water caused cancer in their children. Lois Gibbs said, "Woburns are happening all over the country today. The only way we can fight this is by working within the system and outside the system in an organized choir of voices."[6] She added, "Twenty years after Love Canal, there is still much we don't know about the health effects of the 77,000 chemicals in commercial use today."[7]

People who lived through the events at Love Canal were still fearful years later. Many had health problems or were worried about their future health. They feared for

L ois Gibbs, right, stands next to Deborah Cerrillo Curry, the former vice president of the Love Canal Homeowners Association, during a press conference in 1998.

their children and grandchildren. One former resident recalled how her son lost part of his hearing after playing at the dumpsite. She said, "They told us they were going to build a park. But what we got was a killer."[8]

In 1998, Lois Gibbs said, "[Love Canal] was horrible stress. It destroys marriages, changes your family, changes your life. . . . It's always like a black cloud that hangs over you, even the most joyous moments. It haunts you forever."[9]

Other Chemical Disasters

DATE	PLACE	DESCRIPTION
1953–1983	Minimata Bay, Japan	Fish are contaminated with mercury after a local plastics company, Chisso Chemical, dumps more than 400 tons of the chemical in the water. Causes symptoms in about 1,500 people and more than 300 deaths.
1974	Flixborough, England	At a plant where Nylon 6 is produced, a highly flammable material called cyclohexane leaks out of a reactor, causing an explosion that kills 28 people and damages 2,000 properties.
1980	Elizabeth, New Jersey	Chemical warehouse catches fire, releasing toxic gases from chemicals, acids, and solvents. Thirty firefighters injured; numerous local residents visited hospitals; schools in the region closed during the fire and resulting explosions.
1982–1983	Times Beach, Missouri	Meramec River overflows banks, spreading contaminated oil that was sprayed on roads to control dust; the oil contains dioxin and other poisonous chemicals; government spends more than $33 million on cleanup; entire town evacuated except for 58 families (300 people).
1984	Bhopal, India	More than 25 tons of toxic gas escapes from a storage tank at the Union Carbide Corporation when a disgruntled employee tries to ruin a batch of chemicals. Causes 3,828 deaths and leaves more than 200,000 people with injuries and disabilities.
1986	Basel, Switzerland	Fire at the Sandoz chemical factory releases highly toxic chemicals (including mercury and parathion) into the Rhine River; nearby factories also dump chemicals into the river. Hundreds of thousands of fish and eels die; water left unsuitable for drinking.

Chapter Notes

Chapter 1. Backyard Hazards

1. Jerauld E. Brydges, "Canal Residents Vow a Tax Strike," *Niagara Gazette*, August 3, 1978, p. 1.

2. Lois Marie Gibbs (as told to Murray Levine), *Love Canal: My Story* (Albany, N.Y.: State University of New York, 1982), pp. 36–37.

3. Andrew J. Hoffman, "An Uneasy Rebirth at Love Canal," *Environment*, March 1995, p. 4.

4. Samuel S. Epstein, M.D., Lester O. Brown, and Carl Pope, *Hazardous Waste in America* (San Francisco: Sierra Club Books, 1982), p. 92.

Chapter 2. Dumping Ground

1. "Background on the Love Canal," Love Canal Collection, n.d., <http://ublib.buffalo.edu/libraries/projects/lovecanal/background_lovecanal.html> (October 2, 1999).

2. Ibid.

3. Samuel S. Epstein, M.D., Lester O. Brown, and Carl Pope, *Hazardous Waste in America* (San Francisco: Sierra Club Books, 1982), p. 94.

4. Ibid., p. 95.

5. Ibid.

6. Lois Marie Gibbs (as told to Murray Levine), *Love Canal: My Story* (Albany, N.Y.: State University of New York, 1982), p. 8.

Chapter 3. Fear and Anger

1. Samuel S. Epstein, M.D., Lester O. Brown, and Carl Pope, *Hazardous Waste in America* (San Francisco: Sierra Club Books, 1982), p. 97.

2. Anne Hillis, Testimony Before the Senate Subcommittee on Toxic Substances & Chemical Wastes, March 28, 1979, Love Canal Collection, Documents Online, <http://ublib.buffalo.edu/libraries/projects/lovecanal/disaster_gif/records/hill2.html> (October 2, 1999).

3. Epstein, Brown, and Pope, p. 98.

4. David Pollak, "Closeup: Hooker Dump Troubles Neighbors in LaSalle," *Niagara Gazette*, October 3, 1976, p. 1.

5. David Pollak, "Dump Seepage Tested: City Needs Plan," *Niagara Gazette*, May 1, 1977, p. 1.

6. Mike Brown, "$400,000 Project Is Asked to Seal Off Love Canal," *Niagara Gazette*, August 10, 1977, p. 1-B.

7. U.S. Environmental Protection Agency, Letter from Lawrence R. Moriarty, Rochester Program Support Branch, to William Librizzi, Toxic Substances Coordinator, October 18, 1977: Love Canal Collection, University Archives, University Libraries, State University of New York at Buffalo.

8. Lois Marie Gibbs (as told to Murray Levine), *Love Canal: My Story* (Albany, N.Y.: State University of New York, 1982), p. 12.

9. Ibid.

10. Ibid., p. 15.

Chapter 4. "I Don't Want to Live Here"

1. Marc Mowrey and Tim Redmond, *Not in Our Backyard: The People and Events That Shaped America's Modern Environmental Movement* (New York: William Morrow and Company, Inc., 1993), p. 202.

2. Lois Marie Gibbs (as told to Murray Levine), *Love Canal: My Story* (Albany, N.Y.: State University of New York, 1982), p. 30.

3. Jerauld E. Brydges, "Canal Residents Vow a Tax Strike," p. 1.

4. Mowrey and Redman, p. 203.

5. Gibbs, p. 39.

6. Ibid., p. 40.

7. Ibid.

8. Mike Brown, "Cheers Greet Word of Relief," *Niagara Gazette*, August 5, 1978, <http://ublib.buffalo.edu/libraries/projects/lovecanal/newspapers/nia_gazette/8-5-781.html> (September 20, 1999).

9. Adeline Gordon Levine, *Love Canal: Science, Politics, and People* (Lexington, Mass.: Lexington Books, 1982), pp. 92–93.

10. Beverly Paigen, et al., "Prevalence of Health Problems in Children Living Near Love Canal," *Hazardous Waste & Hazardous Waste Materials*, Vol. 2, No. 2, 1985, pp. 209–223.

11. Anne Hillis, Testimony Before the Senate Subcommittee on Toxic Substances & Chemical Wastes, March 28, 1979, Love Canal Collection, Documents Online, <http://ublib.buffalo.edu/libraries/projects/lovecanal/disaster_gif/records/hill2.html> (October 2, 1999).

12. Ibid.

13. Loretta Gambino, Testimony Before the Senate Subcommittee on Toxic Substances & Chemical Wastes, April 5, 1979, Love Canal Collection, Documents Online, <http://ublib.buffalo.edu/libraries/projects/lovecanal/disaster_gif/records/gambi1.html> (September 19, 1999).

14. Mr. and Mrs. Joseph Dunmire, Letter to the Editor, "Every mother is scared to death," *Niagara Gazette*, April 27, 1980.

15. John Omicinski, "Carey Urges Permanent Relocation of 710 Canal Families," *Niagara Gazette*, May 24, 1980, p. 1.

16. Ibid.

17. E. Willard Miller and Ruby M. Miller, *Contemporary World Issues: Environmental Hazards: Toxic Wastes and Hazardous Material* (Santa Barbara, Calif.: ABC-CLIO, 1991), pp. 19–21.

18. Marie Pozniak, Testimony Before the Senate Subcommittee on Toxic Substances & Chemical Wastes, May 3, 1979, Love Canal Collection, Documents Online, <http://ublib.buffalo.edu/libraries/projects/lovecanal/disaster_gif/records/pozni1.html> (September 20, 1999).

Chapter 5. "A Black Cloud"

1. "After 17 Years, Love Canal Case Settled," CNNfn (The Financial Network), fn Archive, December 21, 1995, <http://www.cnnfn.com/news> (December 13, 1999).

2. Ibid.

3. Verlyn Klinkenborg, "Back to Love Canal: Recycled Homes, Rebuilt Dreams," *Harpers Magazine*, March 1991, p. 27.

4. "Despite Toxic History, Residents Return to Love Canal," CNN (Cable News Network), August 7, 1998, <http://cnn.com/US/9808/07/love.canal/index.html> (November 3, 1999).

5. Ibid.

6. Jean Mikle, "Movie Hits Home for Cancer Fighters," *Asbury (MA) Park Press*, January 10, 1999, reprinted at TEACH (Toxic Environment Affects Children's Health) <http://tr-teach.org/resources/news/19990110.html> (September 2, 1999).

7. Lois Gibbs, "The Legacy of Love Canal," *Boston Globe*, August 7, 1998.

8. Samuel S. Epstein, M.D., Lester O. Brown, and Carl Pope, *Hazardous Waste in America* (San Francisco: Sierra Club Books, 1982), p. 122.

9. Anita Srikameswaran, "Memories Haunt Love Canal Veterans," *Pittsburgh Post-Gazette*, September 19, 1998.

by-products—Materials that are left over after goods are produced.

chromosomes—The genetic material inside cells that carries genetic traits.

corrosive wastes—Acids and other wastes that can eat away at metal, skin, and other materials.

Environmental Protection Agency (EPA)—Federal agency set up in 1970 to set standards for clean air, water, and soil; enforce rules; promote safe ways to dispose of wastes; and monitor cleanup operations.

hazardous waste—Waste material that poses a threat to human health or the environment when it is improperly handled.

ignitable wastes—Waste products that are flammable.

landfill—Underground dumpsite for waste disposal.

radioactive wastes—Waste products that send out rays that can damage human cells.

reactive wastes—Waste products that may explode or release deadly gases when they become hot or are mixed with water or other substances.

toxic wastes—Poisonous chemical wastes that may cause various health problems or death.

Further Reading

Amos, Janine. *Pollution.* Austin, Tex.: Raintree Steck-Vaughn Publishers, 1993.

Gibbs, Lois. *Love Canal, the Story Continues.* Philadelphia, Pa.: New Society Publishers, 1998.

Harlow, Rosie and Morgan, Sally. *Pollution & Waste.* New York, N.Y.: Larousse Kingfisher Chambers, Incorporated, 1995.

Patten, John M. Jr. *Toxic Wastes.* Vero Beach, Fla.: The Rourke Book Company, Incorporated, 1995.

Thompson, Gare. *Take Care of Our Earth.* Austin, Tex.: Raintree Steck-Vaughn Publishers, 1998.

Zipko, Stephen J. *Toxic Threat: How Hazardous Substances Poison Our Lives.* Parsippany, N.J.: Silver Burdett Press, 1990.

Internet Addresses

Center for Health, Environment, and Justice
http://www.chej.org

Ecumenical Task Force of the Niagara Frontier
Love Canal Collection
http://ublib.buffalo.edu/libraries/projects/lovecanal

U.S. Environmental Protection Agency (EPA)
Superfund Program
http://www.epa.gov/superfund

Index

Index